Any Time TEMPTATIONS SERIES

Sanjeev Kapoor's

VEGETARIAN
Snacks
&
STARTERS

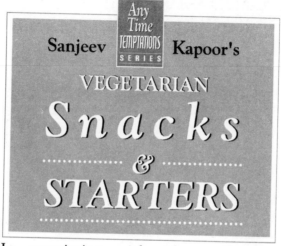

Sanjeev **Any Time TEMPTATIONS SERIES** Kapoor's

VEGETARIAN
Snacks
&
STARTERS

In association with Alyona Kapoor

Popular Prakashan

POPULAR PRAKASHAN PVT. LTD.
35-C, Pt. Madan Mohan Malaviya Marg
Tardeo, Mumbai-400 034.

© 2002 by Sanjeev Kapoor

First Published 2002

(3808)

ISBN - 81-7991-062-8

PRINTED IN INDIA
By Akshar Pratiroop Pvt. Ltd., 201 India Printing House, Wadala
Lower Parel, Mumbai and Published by Ramdas Bhatkal
for Popular Prakashan Pvt. Ltd.
35-C, Pt. Madan Mohan Malaviya Marg,
Tardeo, Mumbai-400 034.

Dedication

This book is dedicated to
all the viewers of Khana Khazana
and my family and friends
who have been a constant support
to me at all times.

Note to the Readers

If variety is the spice of life, it's a delightfully scrumptious world for the vegetarians! For the choice of snacks offered to them is as varied as the colours of the rainbow. This book is a part of the series of 'Any Time Temptations'. All the recipes have been picked out from my earlier books and segregated. Vegetable Spring Rolls and *Samosa* would be comforting to be around as they have become everyday fare for most palates. But then, cooking is an art that has to be mastered and this book will gently guide you through a gamut of new and easy vegetarian snacks to enthrall your family and friends with!

Fluffy *Dhokla* and *Sabudana Wada* have become a focal point. And if one happens to be on the look-out for popular Mumbai fare, the search ends here with *Pav Bhaji*, *Batata Wada*, *Kothimbir Wadi* and what have you!

For those who crave pizzas the choice between the Cajun Vegetable Pizza and the Healthy Pizza would be difficult. Another healthy choice would be the Falafel from the Middle East that could well be in competition with the Indian *Khandvi*, *Mirchi Vada* and *Idlis*.

And if you love bread and its incarnations there are some crunchies like the French Bread Crispies, Sesame Corn Toast, Apple and Cheese Toast or the Chilli Cheese Toast. Have them for breakfast or afternoon tea, serve them to guests as 'small eats' at a party. The choices are difficult to make no doubt!

All the recipes serve four and form part of a menu.

In case you desire to accompany these superb snacks with a dip…simply use the special section on dips and sauces. Vegetarian starters might need a little bit of innovation to present but hardly any motivation to be demolished!

Acknowledgements

A. I. Kazi
Aditi Mehta
Afsheen Panjwani
Anand Bhandiwad
Anil Bhandari
Blue Cilantro, Mumbai
Brijesh Lohana
Capt. K. K. Lohana
Debasis Sikdar
Drs. Meena & Ram Prabhoo
Ganesh Pednekar
Grain of Salt, Kolkata
Harpal Singh Sokhi
Jaideep Chaubal
Jijesh Gangadharan
Jyotsna & Mayur Dvivedi
Lohana Khaandaan

Meghana Samant
Namrata & Sanjiv Bahl
Neelima Acharya
Neena Murdeshwar
Pooja & Rajeev Kapoor
Rajeev Matta
Rajneesh Sharma
Rutika Samtani
Shivani Ganesh
Smeeta Bhatkal
Sunit Purandare
Swapna Shinde
The Yellow Chilli, Jalandhar
The Yellow Chilli, Ludhiana
Tripta Bhagattjee
Uma Prabhu

CONTENTS

GRILLED PANEER WITH HONEY CHILLI SAUCE

INGREDIENTS

Cottage cheese (*paneer*) .. 400 gms
Butter .... 2 tbsps
For the sauce
Garlic .... 8-10 cloves
Onion .... 1 medium sized
Cornstarch .... 1 tbsp
Oil.......... .... 2 tbsps
Red chilli flakes................... 1 tsp
Soy sauce .... 1 tbsp
Honey .... 2 tbsps
Pepper powder .... ¼ tsp
Salt .... to taste

Masala
Red chillies whole 3-4
Coriander seeds .... 1 tsp
Cumin seeds .... ½ tsp
Peppercorns....................... 3-4
Cinnamon .... ½ inch stick
Cloves 3
Nutmeg powder............. a pinch
Oil .... 1 tbsp
Ginger paste .... 1 tsp
Garlic paste .... 1 tsp

METHOD OF PREPARATION

1 Cut the *paneer* into finger sized pieces. Peel, wash and crush the garlic cloves. Peel, wash and chop onion.

2 Blend cornstarch in a quarter cup of water.

3 Prepare the *masala* by roasting whole red chillies, coriander seeds, cumin seeds, peppercorns, cinnamon, cloves and nutmeg on a *tawa* and grind to a coarse powder. Mix it with oil, ginger paste and garlic paste.

4 Heat *tawa*/griddle, put butter and roast the *paneer* on it till it attains a nice brown colour on all sides. You can achieve the same results in a sandwich toaster.

5 For the sauce, heat oil in a pan, add crushed garlic and stir for half a minute. Then add chopped onion, red chilli flakes, prepared *masala*, soy sauce and honey and stir for a few minutes. Add the blended cornstarch. Bring to a boil and cook until the sauce thickens. Season with salt and pepper.

6 Serve the grilled *paneer* hot, accompanied with honey chilli sauce.

FRIED
MOZZARELLA

INGREDIENTS

Mozzarella cheese.......... 400 gms
Eggs...2
Refined flour (*maida*) .... ½ cup
Salt .... to taste

Peppercorns (crushed) .... ¼ tsp
Breadcrumbs .... 1 cup
Oil ....to deep fry
Parsley .... a few sprigs

METHOD OF PREPARATION

1   Cut the mozzarella cheese into one-inch squares with half-inch thickness. Gently pat off any excess moisture with kitchen paper.
2   Mix the eggs lightly and keep aside.
3   Season the flour with salt and freshly crushed peppercorns.
4   Spread the seasoned flour on one plate and bread crumbs on another plate.
5   Press the cheese slices into the flour, coating them evenly with a thin layer of flour. Shake off any excess.

6   Dip them into the egg, then roll them in breadcrumbs. Repeat this process once more.
7   Heat sufficient oil in a *kadai* or wok to a smoking point and fry the cheese slices until golden brown. Drain onto an absorbent kitchen paper.
8   Serve hot immediately (as mozzarella has a tendency of melting fast) garnished with sprigs of parsley.

GREEN PEAS COCONUT TIKKI

INGREDIENTS

Green peas (shelled) .... 1 cup
Coconut (scraped) .... ½ cup
Potatoes .... 4 large sized
Fresh coriander leaves ...... ½ cup
Ginger .... 1 inch piece
Green chillies 3
Oil......... 2 tbsps + to shallow fry

Cumin seeds .... 2 tsps
Asafoetida .... a pinch
Salt .... to taste
Lemon juice .... 1 tsp
Coriander & Mint Chutney ....
.... as required

METHOD OF PREPARATION

1   Boil, cool, peel and mash the potatoes. Add salt, knead till smooth and keep aside.

2   Wash and boil the green peas. When cool, mash them slightly. Clean, wash and finely chop the coriander leaves. Scrape the ginger, wash

and finely chop. Remove stem, wash and finely chop the green chillies.

3   Heat oil in a pan, add cumin seeds, asafoetida, chopped ginger, chopped green chillies and boiled green peas and a little salt. Stir-fry for two to three minutes. Add a little lemon juice and spread on a plate to cool.

4   Add chopped coriander leaves and scraped coconut and mix.

5   Take a portion of mashed potatoes in damp palms, make a dent in the center, fill it with coconut and peas mixture and close in the edges to enclose the stuffing. Press gently and roll the edges to smoothen the sides. Keep them in the refrigerator for five to seven minutes.

6   Heat a little oil on a *tawa* and shallow fry the tikkis on low heat until they turn light brown or till they become crisp.

7   Serve the *tikkis* hot with Coriander and Mint Chutney.

Note: Refer page no. 103 for the recipe of Coriander and Mint Chutney.

ALOO PANEER ROLLS

INGREDIENTS

Potatoes .... 2 large sized
Cottage cheese (*paneer*) .. 200 gms
Raisins (*kishmish*) .... 1 tbsp
Fresh coriander leaves ..... 4 tbsps
Onion .... 1 medium
Green chillies 3-4
Oil................ 1 tbsp + to deep-fry

Red chillies (crushed) ...... ½ tbsp
Garam masala powder .... 1 tsp
Salt .... to taste
Refined flour (*maida*) ...... 4 tbsps
Pepper powder .... ¼ tsp
Milk .... ½ cup
Bread crumbs .... 1 cup

METHOD OF PREPARATION

1 Boil, cool, peel and mash the potatoes (make sure that you don't put boiled potatoes in cold water for cooling. Excess moisture will not dry off easily and handling mashed potato will become slightly difficult).

2   Grate the *paneer*. Soak raisins in warm water for some time before use. Wash and chop coriander leaves. Peel, wash and chop onion. Remove stem, wash and chop green chillies. Season refined flour with a little salt and pepper powder.

3   Heat one tablespoon of oil in a frying pan and sauté chopped onion till transculent.

4   Mix together *paneer*, potatoes, crushed red chillies, fried onion, chopped green chillies, chopped coriander leaves, *garam masala* powder, salt and raisins.

5   Make cylindrical shaped croquettes.

6   Roll the croquettes in seasoned refined flour, then dip in milk and roll in the breadcrumbs. Keep the *aloo paneer* croquettes in the refrigerator for an hour or more.

7   Heat sufficient oil in a *kadai* and deep fry the rolls till golden brown and drain onto an absorbent kitchen towel.

8   Serve hot with Coriander and Mint Chutney.

Note: Refer page no. 103 for the recipe of Coriander and Mint Chutney.

CHEF'S TIP
Fry one piece in the beginning to check the binding of the mix and whether the oil is sufficiently hot.

RED COLESLAW IN PITA POCKETS

INGREDIENTS

Red cabbage ..... ½ medium sized
Onions .... 2 small sized
Red radish 2
Red apples .... 2 medium sized
Lemon juice .... 1 tbsp

Low fat cheese spread ..... 3 tbsps
Skimmed milk yogurt ..... 3 tbsps
Salt .... to taste
Pepper powder .... ½ tsp
Pita bread .... 4 medium sized

METHOD OF PREPARATION

1 Wash and shred cabbage. Peel, wash and thinly slice onions and radish.
2 Peel, wash, core and grate the apples. Mix the sliced vegetables, grated apple and lemon juice together in a bowl.
3 Add the cheese spread, skimmed milk yogurt, salt and pepper and mix well. Divide the red coleslaw into eight equal portions.
4 Warm the pita bread on a griddle plate or a preheated oven. Cut each pita bread into two and fill each half with a portion of red coleslaw.
5 Serve with a sauce or chutney of your choice.

APPLE AND CHEESE TOAST

INGREDIENTS

Apples .... 2 large sized
Lemon juice .... 1 tbsp
Cashewnuts 8
Orange juice .... ½ cup

Whole wheat bread .... 4 slices
Low-fat cottage cheese ... 120 gms
Cinnamon powder .... ½ tsp
Honey .... 1 tbsp

METHOD OF PREPARATION

1 Peel, core and cut the apples into thick slices. Sprinkle lemon juice on apple slices.

2 Toast the cashewnuts in a pan or in a preheated oven till light golden, cool and crush coarsely.

3 Heat a non-stick pan and gently poach the apple slices in the orange juice for about ten minutes or until just soft, turn them over carefully for even cooking.

4 Toast the bread slices, trim the sides.

5 Grate the cottage cheese and mix with the crushed cashewnuts thoroughly.

6 Spread this mixture on the toasted bread slice and arrange the cooked apple slices on top.

7 Sprinkle cinnamon powder and place under a hot grill or in a preheated oven (180°C) until browned to light golden.

8 Drizzle the honey on the hot toasts, cut to desired shape and serve.

FALAFEL

INGREDIENTS

Chickpeas (*kabuli chana*) .... 1 cup
Fresh coriander leaves ..... 2 tbsps
Parsley .... 2 tbsps
Spring onion greens ... 4-5 leaves
Garlic .... 2-3 cloves
Breadcrumbs .... ¼ cup

Soda bicarbonate.. a small pinch
Cumin powder .... ½ tsp
Salt .... to taste
Pepper powder .... ¼ tsp
Paprika .... ½ tsp
Oil .... to deep fry

METHOD OF PREPARATION

1   Wash and soak chickpeas overnight. Drain and dry on a kitchen towel.
2   Clean, wash and chop coriander leaves and parsley.
3   Wash and chop the greens of spring onion. Peel, wash and chop garlic.
4   Grind the chickpeas along with chopped garlic, coriander leaves, parsley, spring onion greens and breadcrumbs in a food processor to a coarse mixture.

5   Add a small pinch of soda bicarbonate. Add the cumin powder and mix well.
6   Season it with salt, pepper powder and paprika. Knead the mixture well and allow it to rest for a couple of hours in a refrigerator.
7   Take the mixture in a tablespoon dampened with water and shape it from top with another damp tablespoon. Many falafels can be shaped like this and stored on a greased plate in a refrigerator prior to frying.
8   Heat sufficient oil in a *kadai* and deep-fry the falafels till golden brown. Drain on a kitchen towel and serve hot. If prepared in advance the unfried falafels can be stored in a refrigerator and fried later.

CHEF'S TIP

It makes a good combination with tabbouleh salad and tahina dip. Falafel is traditionally made with fava beans but you can use chickpeas instead.

HOT AND SOUR IDLIS

INGREDIENTS

Pigeon pea split (*arhar dal*) 1 cup
Rice .... 1 cup
Red chillies whole 6
Tamarind pulp .... 2 tbsps
Jaggery (grated) .... 1 tbsp

Asafoetida .... one large pinch
Turmeric powder .... ½ tsp
Salt .... to taste
Onions .... 2 small sized

METHOD OF PREPARATION

1   Pick, wash and soak the *dal* and the rice separately in three cups of water for four to six hours. Drain and keep aside. Do not mix. Grind the red chillies and tamarind to a fine paste.

2   Grind *dal* smoothly and rice coarsely separately. Mix them thoroughly.

3   Add the paste of red chillies and tamarind, grated jaggery, asafoetida, turmeric powder and salt and mix well. Leave it aside for four to

five hours to ferment.

4   Peel, wash and finely chop onions.
5   Grease the *idli* moulds. Heat a little water in a steam pot.
6   Pour the batter into the moulds, sprinkle the chopped onions on top and steam for about fifteen to twenty minutes or till done.
7   Serve hot with a chutney of your choice.

CHEF'S TIP

Though these *idlis* are quite different from traditional *idlis* made from rice and *urad dal*, they are equally tasty. As these *idlis* have tamarind, chillies and jaggery, you can eat them as an any time snack.

FRENCH BREAD CRISPIES

INGREDIENTS

Whole meal French bread/loaf ... 1
Tomatoes .... 3 large sized
Garlic .... 5–6 cloves
Fresh basil .... a few leaves
Olive oil .... 2 tbsps

Salt .... to taste
Peppercorns (crushed) .... 1 tsp
Red chilli flakes .... ½ tsp
Dry oregano .... a pinch

METHOD OF PREPARATION

1   Cut whole meal French loaf diagonally into half inch thick slices. Wash and finely chop tomatoes. Peel and chop garlic.
2   Clean and wash fresh basil leaves. Chop half of the leaves and cut the remaining leaves into thin strips and keep them in cold water.
3   Apply a little olive oil on the bread slices and toast in a preheated oven or salamander till they become slightly crisp.

4 Mix the chopped tomatoes with garlic, chopped basil and remaining olive oil.

5 Season it with salt, crushed peppercorns, red chilli flakes and dry oregano. Mix it thoroughly.

6 Spread this mixture on the toasted brown bread and transfer it once again to the preheated oven or salamander. Cook till bread starts to become golden brown at the edges.

7 Serve immediately garnished with fresh basil strips.

CHILLI TACOS

INGREDIENTS

Lettuce (preferably iceberg) .... ½ bunch
Spring onions 2
Green chillies 2
Mint leaves .... a few sprigs
Cherry tomatoes 8
Low fat cheese .... ½ cup
Cheddar cheese................. ½ cup

Taco shells 8
Baked beans in tomato sauce .... 1 cup
Chilli sauce.......................... 2 tsps
Lemon juice .... 2 tbsps
Salt .... to taste
Pepper powder .... ½ tsp

METHOD OF PREPARATION

1 Wash the lettuce well under running water and shred. Peel and chop the onions. Wash, slit into two, deseed and finely chop green chillies. Clean, wash and chop half the mint leaves keeping aside the rest for garnish.

2 Wash and quarter the cherry tomatoes. Grate the low fat cheese and cheddar cheese separately.

3   Warm the taco shells in a preheated oven for a few minutes.
4   In a bowl take the baked beans and add grated low fat cheese, chopped onions, chilli sauce, lemon juice and chopped mint leaves. Add salt and pepper powder, mix lightly.
5   Fill the taco shells with shredded lettuce leaves spread evenly and then with the baked beans mixture till the shells are about three-fourth full.
6   Top the shells with grated cheddar cheese, quartered cherry tomatoes and a sprig of mint.
7   Serve immediately.

CHEF'S TIP

Though the taco shells are fried, as the quantity of salad used is more, it becomes a healthy meal with controlled calories.

CAJUN POTATOES

INGREDIENTS

Potatoes .... 8-10 medium sized	Oregano (dried) .... ½ tsp
Lettuce leaves 4	Salt .... to taste
Kashmiri red chilli powder .... 1 tsp	Oil .... 2 tbsps
Red chilli flakes .... 1½ tsps	Butter .... 2 tbsps
Peppercorns (crushed) .... ½ tsp	Lemon juice .... 1 tbsp
Thyme (dried) .... ½ tsp	

METHOD OF PREPARATION

CHEF'S TIP

Instead of roasting in an oven you can cook Cajun potatoes by shallow frying in a pan.

1 Preheat the oven to 200°C. Wash lettuce leaves.
2 Wash the potatoes and cut them into wedges with the skin.
3 Make a marinade of red chilli powder, red chilli flakes, crushed peppercorns, thyme, oregano, salt and oil. Apply the marinade to the potato wedges and keep aside for five to seven minutes.
4 Roast them in the oven, basting with butter, turning them frequently, till golden brown in colour and cooked. Remove and add juice of lemon.
5 Serve them hot on a bed of lettuce leaves.

CHILLI CHEESE TOAST

INGREDIENTS

Bread	8 slices	Onion	1 medium sized
Cheese (grated)	1½ cups	Capsicum (optional)	1 medium sized
Green chillies	4-6	Peppercorns (crushed)	1 tsp
Fresh coriander leaves	½ cup	Salt	to taste

METHOD OF PREPARATION

1. Remove stem, wash and finely chop the green chillies. Clean, wash and chop coriander leaves. Peel, wash and chop onion. Wash, halve, deseed and chop capsicum.
2. In a bowl, mix cheese, green chillies, coriander leaves, onion, capsicum, crushed peppercorns and salt. Divide the mixture into eight equal portions.
3. Toast the bread slices on one side on a tawa.
4. Apply the cheese mixture on the non-toasted side of the bread slices.
5. Grill in a preheated oven (180° C) until the cheese melts and turns golden brown.
6. Cut each slice diagonally into two and serve hot with sauce of your choice.

PIQUANT POTATOES IN JACKETS

INGREDIENTS

Potatoes .... 4 large sized	Coriander powder .... 2 tsps
Onion .... 1 small sized	Turmeric powder .... ½ tsp
Ginger .... 1 inch piece	Garlic salt .... 1 tsp
Garlic .... 3-4 cloves	Pepper powder .... ½ tsp
Fresh coriander leaves ...... a few sprigs	Salt .... to taste
Oil............................... 1 tbsp	Yogurt .... 1 cup
Cumin seeds .... 1 tsp	

METHOD OF PREPARATION

1 Wash and prick the potatoes with a fork and bake in a preheated oven at 190°C for forty minutes or till done.
2 Cut the potatoes in half and scoop out the flesh without spoiling the skin. The skin of the potato is popularly known as the jacket.

3   Peel, wash and finely chop onions. Peel and finely chop ginger and garlic. Wash, dry and chop the coriander leaves.

4   Heat oil in a pan. Add cumin seeds, chopped onion, ginger and garlic. Sauté for a minute.

5   Add the scooped potatoes, coriander powder, turmeric powder, garlic salt and pepper powder.

6   Cook further on medium heat for two minutes, stirring occasionally. Cool slightly and mix in half a cup of well beaten yogurt.

7   Spoon the mixture back into the potato jackets and top each with a tablespoonful of the remaining yogurt. Garnish with chopped coriander and serve hot.

MUSHROOM AND PANEER KABAB

INGREDIENTS

Button mushrooms 14-16	Oil .... 2 tsps
Cottage cheese (*paneer*) .... 200 gms	Red chilli flakes .... 1 tsp
Onions .... 3 medium sized	Honey .... 2 tsps
Capsicums .... 2 large sized	Cumin powder .... 1 tsp
Cherry tomatoes 18-20	*Garam masala* powder .... 1 tsp
Green chillies 2-3	Salt .... to taste
Ginger .... 2 inch piece	Lemon juice .... 2 tsps
Garlic .... 8-10 cloves	*Chaat masala* .... 1 tsp

METHOD OF PREPARATION

1   Clean mushrooms. Cut the *paneer* into one and half inches sized cubes. Peel, wash and cut onions into one inch sized chunks. Wash, halve, remove seeds and cut capsicum into one inch sized pieces. Wash cherry tomatoes.

2 Wash, deseed and roughly chop the green chillies. Peel ginger and garlic and grind them to a paste along with green chillies.

3 In a bowl mix together oil, ginger-garlic and green chilli paste, red chilli flakes, honey, cumin powder, *garam masala* powder, salt, lemon juice and *chaat masala*.

4 Marinate the cottage cheese, button mushrooms, cherry tomatoes, capsicums and onion chunks in this mixture for about an hour.

5 Take eight inches long wooden satay sticks or skewers and soak them in water for half an hour. Remove from water and thread marinated *paneer* cubes, mushrooms, cherry tomatoes, capsicum and onion pieces one after the other on the sticks or skewers.

6 Cook on an open charcoal fire or directly over gas flame for five minutes, rotating the stick for even cooking. Alternatively cook in a preheated oven (180°C) for about fifteen minutes.

STUFFED CHILLIES

INGREDIENTS

Large green chillies	12-16	Cumin powder	½ tsp
Onion	1 medium sized	Red chilli powder	½ tsp
Spinach	½ bunch	Salt	to taste
Fresh mushrooms	½ cup	Breadcrumbs	¼ cup
Processed cheese	50 gms	Oil	for greasing the baking dish
Oil	1 tsp		

METHOD OF PREPARATION

1. Wash and slit the green chillies carefully only on one side, remove seeds and keep aside. Peel, wash and finely chop the onion.
2. Wash the spinach thoroughly under running water. Remove stems, blanch in boiling water for a minute and take out immediately. Refresh in cold water, drain and chop the blanched spinach.
3. Wash and chop the mushrooms. Grate cheese and keep it aside.
4. Heat oil in a pan on medium heat, add chopped onions and cook,

stirring continuously till onions turn light golden brown. Add the chopped mushrooms and cook for another two to three minutes, stirring frequently.

5   Add the blanched spinach and cook for another two minutes. Add cumin powder, red chilli powder and salt. Mix well.

6   Remove from heat and cool. Add breadcrumbs and grated cheese to the mixture.

7   Stuff the green chillies with the spinach and mushroom mixture and bake in a preheated oven at 200°C for about twenty minutes or until the chillies are softened.

8   Serve hot.

VEGETABLE SPRING ROLLS

INGREDIENTS

Onion	1 medium sized	Salt	to taste
Carrots	2 medium sized	Bean sprouts	¾ cup
Capsicum	1 medium sized	Cornstarch	1 cup
Cabbage	½ small sized	**Spring roll wrapper**	
Spring onions	2	Refined flour	¼ cup
Oil	2 tbsps + to deep fry	Cornstarch	1 cup
Soy sauce	1 tbsp	Eggs	2
White pepper powder	¼ tsp	Salt	to taste

METHOD OF PREPARATION

1   Peel, wash, halve and thinly slice onion. Wash, peel and cut carrots intojulienne. Wash, halve, remove stem, deseed and cut capsicum into julienne. Wash, remove core and finely shred cabbage. Wash, trim, halve and thinly slice spring onions along with the greens.

2   Heat oil in a wok or a pan, add sliced onion and carrot, stir fry briefly. Add

45

capsicum and shredded cabbage. Continue stir frying for a minute and add soy sauce, white pepper powder and salt to taste.

3 Add bean sprouts and sliced spring onions along with its greens. Cook for about half a minute, stirring frequently. Remove and cool to bring it to room temperature.

4 Blend one tablespoon cornstarch in half a cup of water.

5 To make spring roll wrappers, mix cornstarch and flour in a mixing bowl, add eggs and salt with two cups of water and whisk thoroughly. Strain through a fine sieve and leave batter aside for fifteen minutes. Adjust the consistency of batter by adding a little water if required.

6 Heat an eight-inch non-stick pan, brush a little oil and pour a ladleful of batter. Swirl the pan to coat the entire surface of the pan and pour back the excess batter.

7 Cook over medium heat, till the edges start curling and peel off or remove spring roll wrapper in one swift motion. Cool and sprinkle a little corn starch. Repeat to make eight to ten wrappers.

8 Divide filling into ten equal portions. Place a portion of filling on one side of the wrapper and roll tightly, folding the sides along and seal the ends with blended cornstarch.

9 Heat sufficient oil in a wok and deep fry two spring rolls at a time in hot oil turning frequently, till they are crisp and golden brown.

10 Drain onto an absorbent kitchen towel and serve hot immediately.

BOMBAY PAV BHAJEE

INGREDIENTS

Potatoes	4 medium sized	Fresh coriander leaves	¼ cup
Tomatoes	4 medium sized	Green peas (shelled)	¼ cup
Cauliflower	¼ small sized	Lemons	2
Onions	2 medium sized	Oil	3 tbsps
Ginger	1 inch	*Pav Bhajee Masala*	1½ tbsps
Garlic	8-10 cloves	Salt	to taste
Capsicum	1 medium sized	Butter	3 tbsps
Green chillies	3-4	*Pav*	8

METHOD OF PREPARATION

1   Boil, cool, peel and grate potatoes. Wash and finely chop tomatoes.
2   Wash and grate cauliflower. Peel, wash and finely chop onions. Peel ginger and garlic. Grind to a fine paste. Wash, halve, remove seeds and finely chop capsicum.
3   Wash, remove stems and finely chop green chillies. Clean, wash and finely chop fresh coriander leaves. Boil green peas in salted

water till soft, drain, mash lightly and keep aside. Cut lemons into wedges.

4 Heat oil in a pan and add three-fourth quantity of chopped onions. Sauté till light brown. Add chopped green chillies and ginger-garlic paste. Stir-fry for half a minute.

5 Add half the quantity of chopped tomatoes and cook on medium heat for three to four minutes, stirring continuously or till oil separates from the *masala*.

6 Add chopped capsicum, boiled and lightly mashed peas, grated cauliflower, grated boiled potatoes and one and half cups of water. Bring it to a boil and simmer for ten minutes, pressing with the back of a spoon a few times, till all the vegetables are completely mashed.

7 Add *Pav Bhajee Masala*, salt and rest of the chopped tomatoes. Cook on medium heat for two minutes, stirring continuously.

8 Heat half of the butter in a thick-bottomed pan or a *tawa*. Slice *pav* horizontally into two and pan-fry in butter for half a minute, pressing two or three times or till *pav* is crisp and light brown.

9 Garnish the *bhajee* with chopped coriander leaves, remaining butter and serve hot with *pav* accompanied with the remaining chopped onions and lemon wedges.

LEHSUNI TIKKI

INGREDIENTS

Potatoes .... 6 medium sized
Salt .... to taste
Onion .... 1 medium sized
Garlic .... 4-6 cloves
Fresh coriander leaves ..... 2 tbsps

Cashewnuts 6-8
Red chilli powder .... ½ tbsp
Cottage cheese (paneer) (grated)
.... ¼ cup
Oil .... to deep fry

METHOD OF PREPARATION

1   Wash and boil the potatoes. Peel and mash them thoroughly. Add
    salt and knead mashed potatoes to make a smooth dough. Divide
    into ten to twelve equal portions.

2   Peel and finely chop the onion and garlic. Clean, wash and finely
    chop fresh coriander leaves.

3   Crush cashewnuts and mix with chopped onion, garlic, coriander
    leaves, red chilli powder, salt and grated paneer. Divide the mixture
    into ten to twelve equal portions.

4   Stuff each portion of mashed potato with a portion of the paneer

mixture. Roll and shape into *tikkis* of approximately two inches diameter and half inch thickness.

5   Heat oil in a *kadai* and deep-fry the *tikkis* to golden brown. Remove and drain on a clean and absorbent kitchen towel or paper.

6   Serve hot with tomato ketchup or Coriander and Mint Chutney.

Note: Refer page no. 103 for the recipe of Coriander and Mint Chutney.

Note: Refer page no. 103 for the recipe of Coriander and Mint Chutney.

CHEF'S TIP

Typically no binding is used in this recipe. However you could add two to three tablespoons of cornstarch to the potato mixture. You may also shallow-fry the *tikkis*.

CAJUN VEGETABLE PIZZA

INGREDIENTS

For pizza base
Refined flour (*maida*) .... 1½ cups
Dried yeast .... 1½ tsps
Sugar .... 1 tsp
Salt .... 1 tsp
Oil .... 1 tbsp
Fat .... for greasing baking tray

For sauce
Tomatoes .... 4 medium sized
Onion .... 1 small
Garlic .... 4-5 cloves
Fresh basil .... a few leaves
Olive oil .... 2 tbsps
Salt .... to taste
Red chillies (crushed) .... 1 tsp

For topping
Tomatoes 4
Onions .... 2 medium sized
Capsicum .... ½ medium sized
Olive oil .... 2 tbsps
Corn kernels .... ½ cup
Oregano (dried) .... ¼ tsp
Fresh basil .... a few leaves
Mozzarella cheese (grated) .... 1½ cups
Red chillies (crushed) .... 1 tbsp

METHOD OF PREPARATION

1 Mix yeast with a quarter cup of warm water and sugar and leave aside until frothy.

2 Add frothy yeast to refined flour. Add salt and oil and mix. Add three-fourth cup of water and knead into a soft dough.

3 Leave the dough covered with a damp cloth in a warm place for about forty-five minutes or until the dough is about double in volume.

4 Knead the dough again and keep for ten to fifteen minutes covered with a moist muslin cloth.

5 Divide pizza dough into four, roll out each portion into medium thick eight inch discs. Prick them with a fork all over. Grease a baking tray with fat and place the pizza base over it. Preheat the oven to 220°C.

6 For the sauce, wash and chop tomatoes finely. Peel, wash and chop onion and garlic. Wash and tear basil leaves into small pieces. Heat olive oil in a pan, add chopped onion and garlic, stir fry briefly and add chopped tomatoes. Add one cup of water and bring it to a boil. Stir in the basil leaves, salt and crushed dried red chillies.

Simmer for about five minutes on medium heat or till it reaches a thick dropping consistency.

7   For pizza topping, wash, halve, de-seed and cut tomatoes into thin strips. Peel, wash and slice onions. Wash, halve, de-seed and cut capsicum into thin strips. Boil corn kernels till cooked.

8   Spread prepared pizza sauce on the pizza dough roundels. Spread half a cup of grated cheese and sprinkle dry oregano. Place the pizza bases on a greased ovenproof tray and bake it in the oven for eight to ten minutes or until the pizza base is crisp.

9   Remove the pizza from the oven and top it with the topping vegetables. Sprinkle crushed red chillies, the remaining grated cheese and olive oil. Tear basil leaves and sprinkle on the pizzas.

10 Again bake the pizzas for a few minutes until the cheese melts and starts bubbling. Remove from the oven, cut each pizza into six or eight pieces and serve hot.

KOTHIMBIR WADI

INGREDIENTS

Fresh coriander leaves ...... 4 cups	Cooking soda .... a pinch
Green chillies 4	Turmeric powder .... ½ tsp
Jaggery (grated) .... 2 tsps	Gram flour (*besan*) .... 1 cup
Salt .... to taste	Oil .... 2 tbsps + to deep fry

METHOD OF PREPARATION

1   Clean, wash and finely chop fresh coriander leaves. Reserve two tablespoons for garnish. Wash, remove stems and finely chop green chillies.

2   Combine chopped fresh coriander leaves, green chillies, jaggery, salt, cooking soda, turmeric powder, gram flour and two tablespoons of oil. Add enough water to make a thick batter. Ensure that the consistency is not too thin.

3 Pour the batter in a greased plate that is at least one and half inches deep or a tray measuring approximately six inches by six inches by one and a half inches.

4 Steam on high heat for fifteen to twenty minutes or till firm and cooked. Check by inserting a skewer into the *wadi* and if it comes out clean, then it is cooked. Remove, cool and cut into one inch sized cubes.

5 Heat sufficient oil in a *kadai* and deep-fry the *wadis* till they are light golden brown in colour and crisp. Drain and keep on an absorbent kitchen towel.

6 Serve hot, garnished liberally with chopped coriander leaves.

Kothimbir Wadi and Bhajanee Thalipeeth

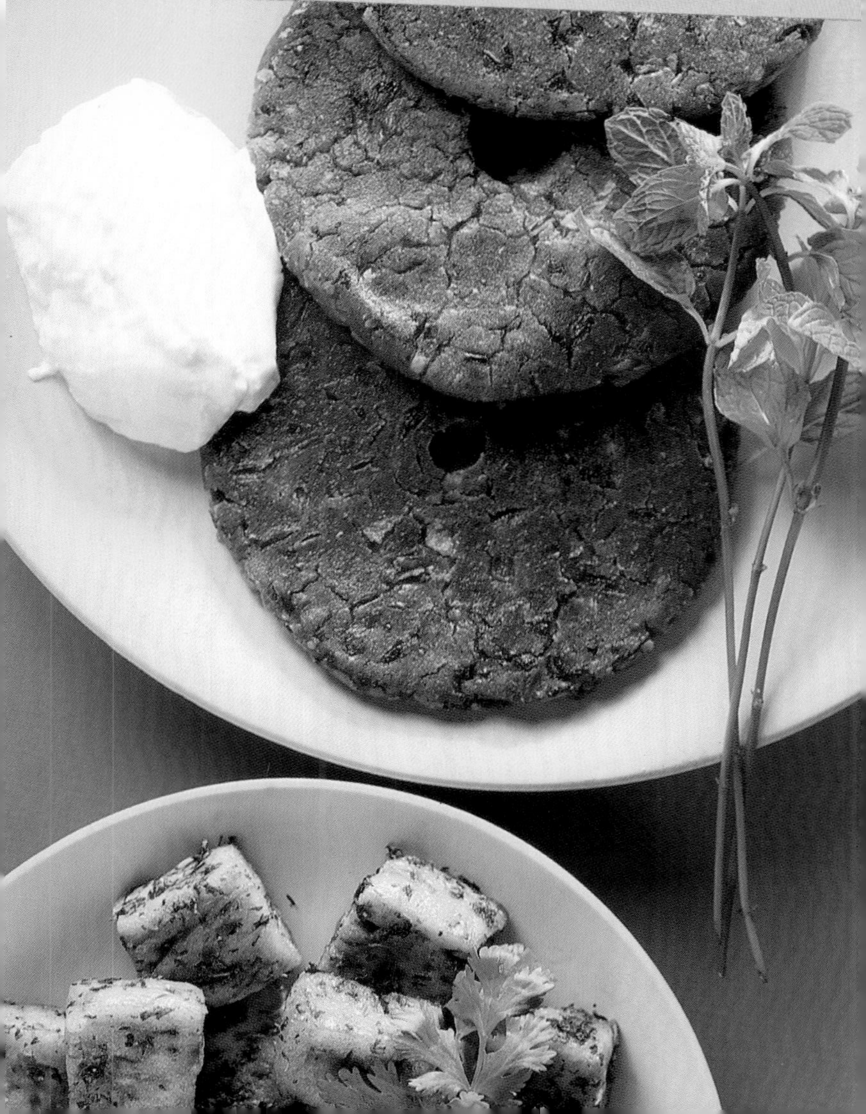

BHAJANEE THALIPEETH

INGREDIENTS

Bhajanee flour	3 cups	Turmeric powder	½ tsp
Onion	1 medium sized	Oil	7 tbsps
Salt	to taste		

METHOD OF PREPARATION

1 Peel, wash and finely chop onion.
2 Add salt, turmeric powder, chopped onion and two teaspoons of oil to the *Bhajanee* flour. Add water as required, a little at a time and knead to form a soft dough.
3 Divide dough into eight equal portions. Flatten each portion on a moist banana leaf or a thick polythene sheet, into quarter inch thick discs of four to five inches diameter.
4 Make a hole in the centre of each *thalipeeth*. Heat a *tawa*, apply a

little oil and transfer *thalipeeth* carefully to the *tawa*. Spoon a little oil on the sides and cook on low heat for one minute.

5 Turn the *thalipeeth* and cook the other side for one minute or till crisp and golden brown.

6 Serve hot with a blob of butter or yogurt.

To make bhajanee flour, dry roast the ingredients, listed below, separately. Cool, mix and grind to a fine powder. It can be stored upto one month.

Whole wheat .... 1 cup
Rice .... 1 cup
Jawar .... 2 cups
Bajra .... 2 cups

Black chana .... ¾ cup
Urad dal .... ¾ cup
Coriander seeds .... ½ cup

CHATPATI TIKKI

INGREDIENTS

Raw bananas .... 2 medium sized
Carrots .... 2 medium sized
Onion .... 1 medium sized
Ginger .... 1 inch piece
Green chillies 3-4
Fresh mint leaves 8-10
Raisins (*kishmish*) 15-20
Dates (seedless) 6

Peanuts (roasted without skin) .... ½ cup
Oil .... 1 tsp
Mustard seeds .... ½ tsp
Black gram split (*urad dal*) ...... ½ tsp
Red chilli powder .... 1 tsp
Chaat masala powder .... 2 tsps
Salt .... to taste
Lemon juice .... 2 tsps

METHOD OF PREPARATION

1   Boil whole raw bananas in sufficient water for fifteen to twenty minutes. Cool, peel and mash well. Wash, peel and grate the carrots. Peel, wash and finely chop onion and ginger.

2   Wash, remove stem and finely chop green chillies. Wash and finely chop mint leaves.

3   Wash raisins, pat dry and chop roughly. Roughly chop seedless dates. Divide this into twelve equal portions. Grind roasted peanuts to a coarse powder.

4   Heat oil in a non-stick pan and add mustard seeds, let them crackle and add *urad dal*. Let it cook till it starts turning brown. Add chopped onion, ginger, garlic and green chillies. Stir-fry for half a minute. Add red chilli powder, mix and quickly add grated carrot.

5   Cook over medium heat for two to three minutes. Sprinkle chopped mint leaves, *chaat masala* powder, mix well and remove from heat.

6   Cool and mix the cooked *masala* with the mashed raw bananas. Add salt to taste, lemon juice and mix well.

7   Divide this mixture into twelve equal portions. Stuff a portion of the date and raisin mixture into each portion of raw banana mixture.

8   Wet your palm and form this mixture into a patty (*tikki*) of not more than half inch thickness.

9   Coat the *tikkis* with coarse peanut powder, pressing them lightly with your palms.

10 Heat a non-stick fry pan or a griddle plate (*tawa*), place the peanut coated *tikkis*. Cook on medium heat till the crust is crisp and nicely brown. Make sure that the *tikkis* are heated through. Serve immediately with a tangy sauce of your choice.

MIRCHI
VADA

INGREDIENTS

Green chillies .... 16 large sized
Potatoes (boiled) ... 6 medium sized
Fresh coriander leaves ...... 3-4 sprigs
Red chilli powder .... 1 tbsp
Garam masala powder 1tbsp
Chaat masala .... 1 tsp
Salt .... to taste

For batter
Gram flour (*besan*) .... 1 cup
Baking powder .... 1 tsp
Red chilli powder .... 1 tbsp
Salt .... to taste
Oil .... for deep-frying

METHOD OF PREPARATION

1 Slit green chillies and remove seeds. Do not remove the stems.
2 Boil the potatoes. Cool, peel and grate them. Clean, wash and finely chop coriander leaves.
3 Add red chilli powder, *garam masala* powder, *chaat masala*, chopped

coriander leaves and salt to the grated potatoes. Mash and mix well. Divide this into sixteen equal portions.

4   Stuff a little of each portion of this mixture into each of the green chillies and also cover the chillies with the remaining potato mixture. Keep them in the refrigerator for about half an hour.

5   Prepare a thick batter using *besan*, baking powder, red chilli powder, salt with around one cup of water. Let the batter stand for ten minutes.

6   Heat oil in a *kadai* to a frying temperature. Dip stuffed green chillies into the *besan* batter and deep fry until golden brown.

7   Drain onto an absorbent paper to remove excess oil and serve hot with a sauce/*chutney* of your choice.

HEALTHY PIZZA

INGREDIENTS

For pizza base
Dried yeast .... 1½ tsps
Sugar .... 1 tsp
Whole wheat flour .... 1½ cups
Soya flour .... 2 tbsps
Salt .... 1 tsp
Olive oil .... 1 tbsp
Wheat bran .... 2 tbsps

For sauce
Tomatoes .... 4 medium sized
Onion .... 1 small sized
Garlic .... 4-5 cloves

Fresh basil .... a few leaves
Olive oil .... 2 tbsps
Salt .... to taste
Red chillies (crushed) .... 1 tsp

For topping
Mushrooms 10-12
Capsicum .... 1 medium sized
Tomatoes .... 2 medium sized
Onion .... 1 medium sized
Low fat mozzarella cheese .... 1 tbsp
Oregano (dried) .... ¼ tsp

METHOD OF PREPARATION

1 Mix yeast with sugar and one teaspoon of warm water and leave aside until frothy.

2   Add frothy yeast to a mixture of whole wheat and soya flour. Add salt, olive oil and wheat bran. Add water and knead into soft dough.

3   Leave the dough covered with a damp cloth in a warm place for about forty-five minutes or until the dough is about double in volume.

4   Divide pizza dough into four, roll out each portion into medium thick eight inch discs. Prick them with a fork all over. Pre-heat an oven to 220°C.

5   For the sauce, wash and chop tomatoes finely. Peel, wash and chop onion and garlic. Wash and tear basil leaves into small pieces. Heat olive oil in a pan, add chopped onion and garlic, stir-fry briefly and add chopped tomatoes. Add one cup of water and bring it to a boil. Stir in the basil leaves, salt and crushed dried red chillies. Simmer for about five minutes on medium heat or till it reaches a thick dropping consistency.

6   For pizza topping, wash mushrooms thoroughly with plenty of water, pat them dry and slice. Wash capsicum, halve to deseed and then cut into thin strips. Wash and cut tomatoes into quarters and cut into thin strips. Peel, wash and slice onion. Grate low-fat mozzarella cheese.

7   Spread prepared pizza sauce on rolled pizza base, top it with sliced onion, sliced mushrooms, tomato and capsicum strips. Finally sprinkle grated low-fat mozzarella cheese to evenly cover the pizza top. Crush dried oregano leaves and sprinkle on the pizza.

8   Place it on a greased ovenproof tray and bake in a preheated oven for about twenty minutes or until the pizza base is crisp and the cheese melts and starts bubbling.

9   Remove from oven, cut into six or eight pieces and serve hot.

CHEF'S TIP

The pizza base can be baked in advance separately and then baked again with the topping on it at the time of consumption.

VEGETABLE SAMOSA

INGREDIENTS

For dough
Refined flour (*maida*) .... 1 cup
Carom seeds (*ajwain*) ...... ½ tbsp
Ghee/oil .... 3 tbsps
Salt .... to taste

For stuffing
Ginger .... 1 inch piece
Green chillies 2
Potatoes .... 4 large sized

Green peas (shelled) .... ½ cup
Oil .... 2 tbsps+to deep fry
Cumin seeds .... 1 tsp
Red chilli powder .... 1 tsp
Salt .... to taste
Dry mango powder (*amchur*) .... 1 tsp
Garam masala powder .... 1 tsp
Fresh coriander leaves ..... 3-4 sprigs

METHOD OF PREPARATION

1 Mix the dough ingredients. Add water little by little and make a stiff dough. Cover it with a damp cloth for ten to fifteen minutes.

2 Peel, wash and finely chop ginger. Wash, de-stem and finely chop green chillies. Peel, wash and cut the potatoes into half-centimeter cubes.

3   Cook green peas in salted boiling water till soft. Refresh in cold
    water. Drain out excess water.
4   Heat oil in a pan, add cumin 'seeds and when they start to change
    colour, add ginger, green chillies and potato cubes.
5   Add red chilli powder, salt, *amchur* and *garam masala* powder. Stir well.
6   Sprinkle water and cook covered till potatoes are done. Add green
    peas and mix well. Let it cool.
7   Divide the dough into sixteen equal portions and roll them into
    balls. Apply a little flour and roll them into four-inch diameter
    elongated diskettes.
8   Cut into half, apply a little water on the edges. Shape into a cone
    and stuff it with the potato and peas filling. Seal the edges.
9   Deep fry in medium hot oil till half done. Drain onto an absorbent
    paper. Just before serving deep fry once again at a higher temperature
    till crisp and golden brown.
10 Serve hot with Tamarind Chutney.

Note: Refer page no. 101 for the recipe of Tamarind Chutney.

RICE PAKORAS

INGREDIENTS

Rice (cooked) .... 2 cups
Gram flour (*besan*) .... ½ cup
Green chillies 3-4
Ginger .... 1 inch piece
Onion .... 1 large sized

Fresh coriander leaves . ¼ bunch
Chaat masala .... 1 tsp
Salt .... to taste
Oil .... to deep fry

METHOD OF PREPARATION

1. Remove stems, wash and finely chop the green chillies. Peel, wash and finely chop the ginger. Peel, wash and finely chop the onion. Clean, wash, finely chop the coriander leaves.
2. Mix all the ingredients, except oil. Add one-fourth cup of water to make a thick batter.
3. Heat oil in a *kadai* to a frying temperature.
4. Spoon the batter into hot oil by using a tablespoon and deep fry till light golden brown.

5 Drain onto an absorbent paper to remove excess oil and fry once again in very hot oil briefly.

6 Drain once again onto an absorbent paper and serve hot with a *chutney* of your choice.

CHEF'S TIP

For this recipe you may also use leftover cooked rice.

SABUDANA VADA

INGREDIENTS

Sago (*sabudana*) .... 1½ cups
Potatoes .... 3 medium sized
Peanuts (roasted) .... 1 cup
Green chillies 3

Fresh coriander leaves .... ¼ bunch
Lemon juice .... 1 tbsp
Salt .... to taste
Oil .... to deep fry

METHOD OF PREPARATION

1   Soak the *sabudana* (in enough water to cover it) for about two hours. Drain out excess water. Boil, cool, peel and mash the potatoes.
2   Coarsely grind the roasted peanuts. Remove stems, wash and finely chop the green chillies.
3   Clean, wash and finely chop coriander leaves.
4   Mix together *sabudana*, potatoes, peanuts, green chillies and coriander leaves, lemon juice and salt. Mix thoroughly.
5   Form into sixteen lemon sized balls, flatten between your palms and deep fry in hot oil till golden brown.
6   Serve hot with *chutney* of your choice.

DHOKLA

INGREDIENTS

Rice .... 1 cup
Black gram split (*urad dal*) .... ¼ cup
Yogurt .... ¼ cup
Warm water .... 1½ cup
Ginger .... 1 inch piece

Green chillies 4
Fresh coriander leaves ..... 3-4 sprigs
Soda bi-carbonate (baking soda) ...... ½ tsp
Lemon juice .... 1 tbsp
Oil .... 2 tbsps

METHOD OF PREPARATION

1　Dry roast the rice and the *dal* on medium heat for four to five minutes. Cool and grind into a semi-coarse powder.

2　Put the powder in a bowl. Add yogurt which should be a little sour and to this add warm water. Mix thoroughly so that no lumps are formed and the batter is of pouring consistency.

3　Add salt and let it ferment for eight to ten hours.

4　Peel and wash ginger. Remove stems and wash the green chillies. Grind them together into a paste. Clean, wash and finely chop coriander leaves.

5 Once fermented, mix the ginger-green chilli paste with the batter.

6 Grease the *dhokla* platter or a *thali*. Boil water in the steamer/boiler.

7 Pour half of the batter in another vessel. In a small bowl, add one-fourth teaspoon soda bi-carbonate, half a teaspoon oil and half teaspoon lemon juice. Add this to the batter and mix well. Repeat this for the remaining batter just before putting it in the steamer.

8 Pour this onto the greased platter and keep it in the steamer to steam for eight to ten minutes.

9 Check with a knife. If the knife comes out clean, it is cooked.

10 Sprinkle some finely chopped coriander leaves and serve hot with Coriander and Mint Chutney.

Note: Refer page no. 103 for the recipe of Coriander and Mint Chutney.

CHEF'S TIP

You can also put crushed peppercorn or red chilli powder over the *dhokla*. It is best enjoyed with *ghee* if desired.

KHANDVI

INGREDIENTS

Gram flour (*besan*) .... 1¼ cups	Lemon juice .... 1 tbsp
Ginger .... 1 inch piece	Oil .... 4 tbsps
Green chillies 2	Mustard seeds .... 1 tsp
Yogurt .... 1 cup	Asafoetida .... a pinch
Salt .... to taste	Coconut (scraped) .... 2 tbsps
Turmeric powder .... ½ tsp	Fresh coriander leaves .... ¼ bunch

METHOD OF PREPARATION

1 Sieve the *besan* and keep in a bowl. Peel and wash ginger. Remove stems and wash green chillies. Grind the two together. Grease the reverse side of a few *thalis* or marble tabletop.
2 Make buttermilk with yogurt and two cups water.
3 Mix the *besan* with ginger-green chillies paste, salt, turmeric powder, lemon juice and buttermilk. Take care that there are no lumps.
4 Cook this mixture till it thickens into a thick batter. Stir constantly.
5 Quickly spread the mixture over the greased inverted *thalis* or

marbled top as thinly as possible while the batter is still hot.

6 When cool, roll the layer towards you and cut into one inch pieces.

7 Heat oil and add mustard seeds. When they crackle, add asafoetida and pour over the pieces.

8 Serve garnished with scraped coconut and chopped coriander leaves.

CHEF'S TIP

Making Khandvi is an art, it takes some practice to get the correct consistency after cooking. Try small portions first.

PATRA

INGREDIENTS

Colocassia leaves (*arbi*) 12
Fresh coriander leaves ...... ½ bunch
Gram flour (*besan*) .... 1½ cups
Turmeric powder .... 1 tsp
Red chilli powder .... 1 tsp
Coriander powder .... 2 tsps
Cumin powder .... 1 tsp
Sesame seeds (crushed) ..... 2 tsps
Salt .... to taste

Green chillies paste .... 1 tsp
Ginger paste .... 1 tsp
Oil .... 4 tbsps
Tamarind pulp .... 2 tbsps
Jaggery .... 100 gms
Mustard seeds .... 1 tsp
Asafoetida .... ¼ tsp
Coconut (scraped) .... ¼ cup

METHOD OF PREPARATION

1 Remove the thick stem from the colocassia leaves. Wash the leaves, pat them dry and keep aside. Clean, wash and finely chop coriander leaves.

2 In a bowl take gram flour, turmeric powder, red chilli powder, coriander powder, cumin powder, crushed sesame seeds, salt, green

chillies paste, ginger paste and two tablespoons of oil and mix well.
3   Add tamarind pulp and grated jaggery and mix well again to make a thick paste.
4   Take one colocassia leaf, spread some of this paste evenly on the back side. Keep another leaf over it and spread the paste similarly. Repeat this once more, using up three leaves. Fold over the two sides and roll, securing the open edge inwards. Tie with a thread.
5   Similarly form three more rolls. Place these rolls on a sieve and steam for thirty to forty minutes or till done. Remove from heat and let them cool.
6   Cut into half-centimetre thick pieces. Heat the remaining oil in a pan. Add mustard seeds. When they crackle add asafoetida and then put in the pieces. Sauté till golden brown.
7   Garnish with scraped coconut and chopped coriander leaves.

SPICED EGGPLANT SAVOURY

INGREDIENTS

Eggplant (brinjal)...........................
1 medium sized (approx. 250 gms)
Garlic .... 5 cloves
Tomatoes .... 3 medium sized
Onion .... 1 medium sized
Green chillies 2-3

Fresh mint leaves .... ¼ cup
Fresh coriander leaves ...... ¼ cup
Lemon juice .... 1 tsp
Salt .... to taste
Oil .... 1 tsp
Brown bread .... 4 slices

METHOD OF PREPARATION

1   Wash eggplant, prick it using a fork.
2   Roast eggplant over direct flame or in a pre-heated oven until soft.
    Cool roasted eggplant, then remove the outer burnt skin completely.
    Wash it well. Drain excess water and chop it fine.
3   Peel and chop garlic. Wash and chop tomatoes. Peel, wash and

chop onion. Wash green chillies, de-stem and chop. Clean, wash mint and coriander leaves and chop them finely.

4   Mix eggplants with onion, tomatoes, garlic, green chillies, fresh coriander leaves, lemon juice and salt.

5   Cook this mixture in a non-stick pan with a little oil on medium heat until it dries well.

6   Toast brown bread slices till crisp. Spread this mixture on the toasted bread pieces. Sprinkle mint leaves on top, cut each slice into two or four pieces. Serve warm, chilled or at room temperature.

CHEF'S TIP

To make it more delicious, grated low-fat mozzarella can be put on top and then put in hot oven until cheese melts and starts bubbling.

STEAMED CRESCENTS

INGREDIENTS

Rice flour	1 cup	Capsicum	1 medium sized
Salt	1 tsp	Bengal gram (chana dal), roasted	¼ cup
Oil	1 tsp	Oil	1 tbsp
For filling		Cumin seeds	½ tsp
Carrot	1 medium sized	Onion seeds (kalonji)	½ tsp
Onion	1 medium sized	Dry mango powder (amchur)	1 tsp
Garlic	6-8 cloves	Salt	to taste
Ginger	1 inch pice		
Green chillies	4-5		

METHOD OF PREPARATION

1 Peel, wash and grate carrot. Peel, wash and chop onion, garlic and ginger as finely as possible. Wash, de-stem and chop green chillies. Wash capsicum, halve, de-seed and chop. Crush roasted *chana dal* lightly.

2 Heat oil in a non-stick pan, add cumin seeds and *kalonji*. Stir-fry briefly. Add onion, garlic, ginger and green chillies and sauté for

three to four minutes.

3   Add capsicum and carrot and continue cooking. Add *chana dal*, *amchur* and salt to taste. Remove from fire and cool.

4   Bring one cup of water to boil in a thick-bottomed non-stick pan. Add one teaspoon of salt and oil. When the water starts boiling, add rice flour in a continuous flow, stirring rapidly to avoid lumps. Cook for two minutes, stirring all along.

5   Remove onto a plate, cover with a damp cloth and let it sweat for a few minutes. Knead with your palm to a smooth dough, cover and keep.

6   Divide the rice dough into sixteen to eighteen equal portions and make them into balls.

7   Lightly oil your palm and spread each ball to approximately three inches round disc, by pressing with your fingers to make it as thin as possible. Place sufficient filling and fold into half moon shape. Press the edges firmly with your fingers to seal.

8   Repeat with the rest of the dough.

9   Heat water in a steam pot and steam vegetable crescents in small batches for about ten to twelve minutes or till completely cooked.

10   Serve straight from the steamer with a hot and spicy sauce of your choice.

PANEER KOLIWADA

INGREDIENTS

Cottage cheese (*paneer*) ... 300 gms
Gram flour (*besan*) .... ½ cup
Cumin powder .... ½ tsp
Yogurt .... 2 tbsps
Kashmiri red chilli powder .... 2 tsps
Salt .... to taste

Ginger paste .... 1 tbsp
Garlic paste .... 1 tbsp
Lemon juice .... 2 tbsps
Oil .... to fry
Chaat masala .... ½ tsp

METHOD OF PREPARATION

1 Cut the *paneer* into finger size pieces three inches by half inch by half inch.
2 Prepare a thick batter with *besan*, cumin powder, yogurt, red chilli powder, salt, ginger paste, garlic paste and lemon juice.
3 Marinate the *paneer* pieces in this batter for half an hour.
4 Heat oil in a *kadai* and deep fry the *paneer* pieces till crisp on the outside.
5 Serve hot, sprinkled with *chaat masala*.

CHEF'S TIP

To make Paneer Koliwada extra crisp, add a tablespoon of cornstarch/cornflour to the batter.

SESAME CORN TOAST

INGREDIENTS

Corn kernels (fresh) .... 1 cup
Capsicum .... 1 medium sized
Onion .... 1 medium sized
Ginger .... 1 inch piece
Garlic .... 4-6 cloves
Green chillies 2-3
Fresh coriander leaves ...... ¼ cup
Potatoes .... 3 medium sized

Soy sauce .... ½ tbsp
Cornstarch .... ¼ cup
White pepper powder .... ½ tsp
Ajinomoto .... ¼ tsp
Salt .... to taste
Bread slices 8
Sesame seeds (toasted) ..... ½ cup
Oil .... to deep-fry

METHOD OF PREPARATION

1 Wash, drain thoroughly and finely mince corn kernels. Wash, halve, deseed and finely chop capsicum. Peel, wash and finely chop onion. Peel and finely chop ginger and garlic.

2 Wash, remove stems, deseed and finely chop green chillies. Clean, wash and finely chop coriander leaves. Boil potatoes in sufficient water, drain, cool, peel and mash them.

3   Add onion, ginger, garlic, green chillies, coriander leaves, soy sauce, two tablespoons of cornstarch, white pepper powder, ajinomoto and salt to corn and potato. Mix thoroughly.

4   Blend the remaining cornstarch in half a cup of water. Cut bread slices with a round cookie cutter to one inch diameter sized pieces.

5   Brush the bread pieces with blended cornstarch and apply a thick layer of the corn mixture and smoothen with wet hands. Sprinkle sesame seeds generously on the pieces and press lightly. Shake off the excess seeds and refrigerate for fifteen minutes.

6   Heat sufficient oil in a wok and deep fry the prepared pieces for two to three minutes, or until crisp and golden brown in colour, turning occasionally.

7   Remove, drain onto an absorbent kitchen towel and serve hot with a sauce of your choice.

Sesame Corn Toast

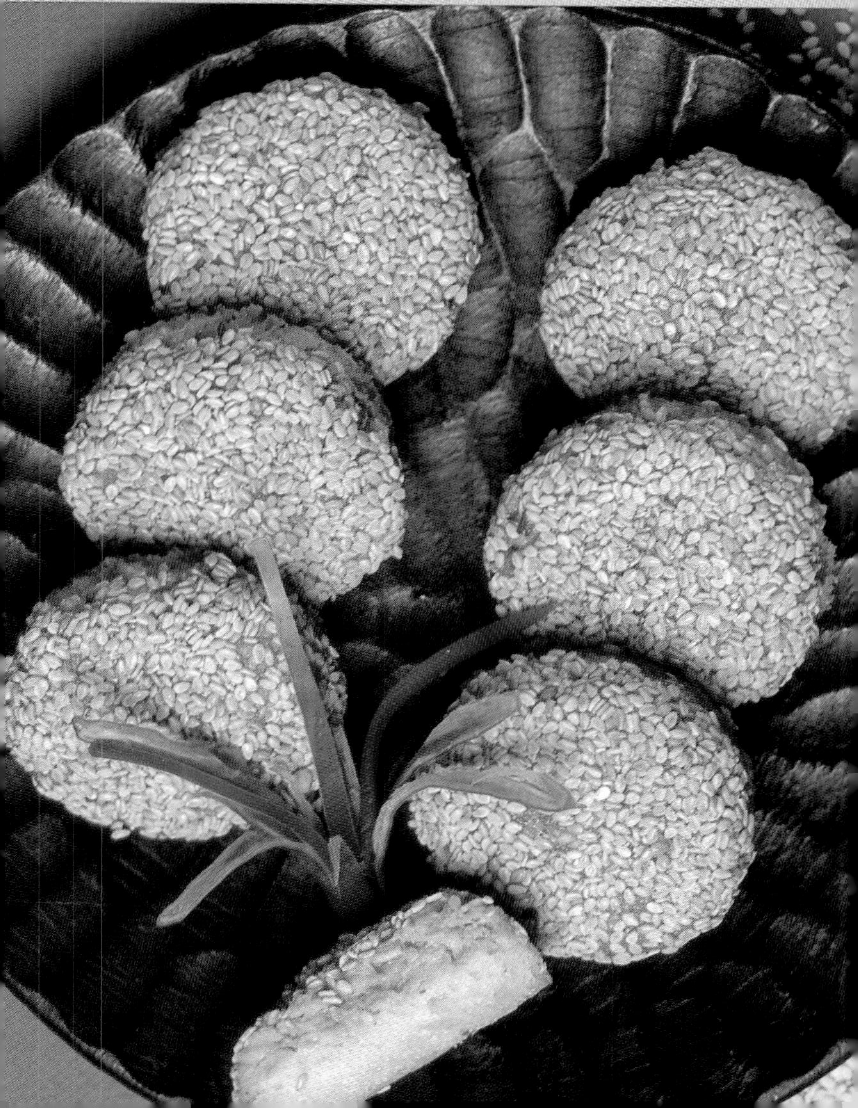

BATATA VADA

INGREDIENTS

Potatoes .... 4-6 medium sized
Green chillies 4
Garlic .... 8-10 cloves
Fresh coriander leaves ...... ¼ cup
Lemon 1
Turmeric powder .... ¼ tsp
Salt .... to taste
Asafoetida .... a pinch

For batter
Gram flour (*besan*) .... 1½ cups
Salt .... to taste
Red chilli powder .... ½ tsp
Turmeric powder .... ¼ tsp
Cooking soda .... a small pinch
Oil .... 1 tbsp+to deep fry

METHOD OF PREPARATION

1 Boil, cool, peel and roughly mash the potatoes.
2 Peel and wash garlic. Remove the stems and wash the green chillies. Grind green chillies and garlic together in a mixer and make a paste. Wash and chop coriander leaves. Squeeze the lemon to extract the juice.
3 In a bowl, add mashed potatoes, garlic-green chilli paste, turmeric

powder, asafoetida, lemon juice, chopped coriander leaves and salt.
4   Make equal sized balls of the above mixture and keep aside.
5   Take gram flour in a bowl, add cooking soda, turmeric powder, red chilli powder and salt. Heat one-tablespoon of oil and add it to the gram flour mixture. Add just sufficient water to make a coating of consistent batter.
6   Heat oil in a *kadai*. Dip the potato mixture balls in the batter and deep fry in hot oil till golden brown in colour. Remove and drain onto an absorbent kitchen towel.
7   Serve hot with *chutney* or sauce of your choice.

SPINACH AND MUSHROOM PANCAKES

INGREDIENTS

Spinach leaves ..... 2 medium bundles	Salt .... to taste
Onion .... 1 medium sized	White pepper powder .... ¼ tsp
Garlic .... 6-8 cloves	Whole wheat flour (*atta*) .. ¾ cup
Fresh mushrooms 10-12	Skimmed milk .... ¾ cup
Oil .... 1 tsp	Carom seeds (*ajwain*) ...... ¼ tsp

METHOD OF PREPARATION

1 Clean and wash the spinach leaves thoroughly. Drain and chop roughly.
2 Peel, wash and chop onion. Peel and chop garlic. Wash and wipe mushrooms with a kitchen towel and chop them.
3 Heat oil in a pan, add garlic, stir-fry briefly. Add onion and

mushrooms and cook till the onion becomes soft and translucent. Cook on high heat so that the excess moisture from the onion and mushrooms dries to some extent.

4 Add chopped spinach, salt and white pepper powder and cook spinach until all the moisture evaporates. Remove from heat and divide the spinach mixture into eight equal portions and keep warm.

5 Mix salt with whole wheat flour and add milk. Whisk well. Add water as required, to make a smooth batter of pouring consistency. Strain the batter if there are lumps.

6 Mix in the *ajwain* and stir well. Rest the batter for at least fifteen minutes.

7 Heat a six inch non-stick pan. Grease with a little oil, if required. Pour half a ladle of batter and spread into a round shape. Cook for half a minute on medium heat, turn over and cook slightly.

8 Spread a portion of cooked spinach on three fourth portion of the pancake and then roll it ensuring that the filling does not spill out.

9 Cook rest of the pancakes in a similar way. Serve immediately.

CHEF'S TIP

The pancakes can be topped with a little low fat cheese and gratinated in a grill just before serving.

CHILLI PANEER

INGREDIENTS

Cottage cheese (*paneer*) 300 gms
Oil .... 2 tbsps + to deep fry
Cornstarch .... 3 tbsps
Onion .... 1 medium sized
Garlic .... 3-4 cloves
Green chillies 6-8

Capsicums .... 2 medium sized
Vegetable stock .... 1 cup
Salt .... to taste
Soy sauce........................... 2 tbsps
Ajinomoto .... ¼ tsp

METHOD OF PREPARATION

1 Cut *paneer* into diamond shaped medium sized pieces. Heat
   sufficient oil in a wok, roll the *paneer* pieces in one tablespoon
   cornstarch and deep fry on medium heat until the edges start to
   turn brown. Remove and drain onto an absorbent kitchen towel.
2 Blend remaining cornstarch in half a cup of water.
3 Peel, wash onion, halve and cut into thick slices. Peel and crush
   garlic. Wash, remove stem and slice green chillies. Wash, halve,

deseed and cut capsicums into thick strips.

4 Heat two-tablespoons of oil in a wok, add garlic and stir fry briefly. Add onion, capsicums, green chillies and continue to stir fry for a couple of minutes.

5 Add *paneer* and stir in vegetable stock. Add salt, soy sauce, ajinomoto and mix well.

6 Add blended cornstarch and cook on high heat stirring and tossing until the sauce thickens to coat the *paneer* and the vegetables. Serve hot immediately.

Note: Refer page no. 104 for the recipe of Vegetable Stock.

CRISPY SPRING ROLLS WITH SWEET CHILLI DIP

INGREDIENTS

Rice vermicelli .... ¼ cup
Ginger .... 1 inch piece
Carrot .... 1 medium sized
Spring onions 2
Spinach .... 8-10 leaves
Fresh coriander leaves .. few sprigs
Egg 1
Oil .... 3 tbsps
Bean sprouts .... ¼ cup
Soy sauce .... 2 tbsps

Spring roll wrappers 10-12
Salt .... to taste
White pepper powder .... ¼ tsp
Ajinomoto (optional) .... ¼ tsp
Oil .... for frying
For the dipping sauce
Sugar .... ¼ cup
Rice vinegar .... ½ cup
Fresh red chillies 2
Salt .... to taste

METHOD OF PREPARATION

1 For the dipping sauce place sugar in a small saucepan with one fourth cup of water. Heat gently, stirring until the sugar dissolves. Boil it gently till it forms a light syrup. Stir in the red chillies, salt and rice vinegar and leave to cool thoroughly.

2 Wash, scrape and chop ginger. Peel, wash and grate carrot. Peel, wash and finely chop white bulbs of the spring onions. Wash and chop spinach and coriander leaves.

3 Break egg, mix lightly and keep aside.

4 Boil vermicelli in sufficient water with one tablespoon of oil till almost cooked, drain, refresh in cold water and keep aside.

5 Heat the remaining oil in a wok, add chopped ginger and stir-fry for fifteen seconds. Add the onion and grated carrots and stir for a few minutes. Add the bean sprouts, spinach, coriander leaves, soy sauce and boiled vermicelli and stir for another minute. Add salt, pepper and ajinomoto and mix. Set aside to cool.

6 Place a spring roll wrapper on the work surface. Put two tablespoons of filling in the middle. Fold over the wrapper to encase the filling

completely.

7   Fold in each side, then roll up tightly. Brush the end with egg to seal (you can use a paste of refined flour and water to replace egg). Repeat until all the filling has been used.

8   Heat oil and deep-fry the spring rolls in batches until golden and crisp. Drain on an absorbent kitchen paper.

9   Serve hot with the sweet chilli dipping sauce.

CHEESE AND HERB DIP

INGREDIENTS

Cheese (grated) .... 1 cup

Milk .... ¼ cup

Salt .... to taste

White pepper powder .... ¼ tsp

Dry oregano .... ¼ tsp

Dry thyme .... ¼ tsp

METHOD OF PREPARATION

1 Mix cheese and milk.

2 Heat this mixture in a double boiler (a pan with wider mouth half filled with heated water into which the pan with cheese and milk will be placed) so that the cheese melts and the mixture gets a smooth consistency.

3 Season with salt, pepper and dry herbs. Use it immediately or else it will thicken again.

PEANUT YOGURT DIP

INGREDIENTS

Yogurt .... 2 cups
Peanuts (roasted) .... ¼ cup
Fresh coriander leaves ..... 2 tbsps

Red chillies whole 2
Salt .... to taste
Cream .... ¼ cup

METHOD OF PREPARATION

1   Hang yogurt overnight in a muslin cloth to remove excess moisture. This process can be carried out in the refrigerator to avoid the yogurt from getting too sour.
2   Clean, wash and finely chop coriander leaves.
3   Crush roasted peanuts coarsely. Remove stem and crush red chillies.
4   Take yogurt in a mixing bowl, whisk it to get a smooth texture.
5   Season with salt, add red chillies and peanuts and coriander leaves. Whisk in the cream and mix well.

SICHUAN SAUCE

INGREDIENTS

Green chillies 2
Spring onions 2
Ginger .... 1 inch piece
Garlic .... 10 cloves
Celery .... 2-3 inches stalk
Red chillies whole 10-12

Oil .... ½ cup
Vegetable stock or water ...... ½ cup
Tomato ketchup .... 3 tbsps
Salt .... to taste
Vinegar .... 2 tsps

METHOD OF PREPARATION

1   Wash, de-stem and finely chop green chillies. Peel, wash and finely chop spring onions. Wash and finely chop some of the spring onion greens. Peel, wash and grate ginger. Peel and finely chop two cloves of garlic. Wash and cut celery stalk into small pieces. Boil whole red chillies in one cup of water for five to seven minutes. Peel the remaining garlic.

2. Grind the whole red chillies and the remaining cloves of garlic to a fine paste.

3   Heat oil, add chopped garlic, green chillies, spring onions and ginger
    and sauté for a minute.
4   Add the red chillies and garlic paste and continue to sauté.
5   Add vegetable stock or water, celery, tomato ketchup, salt and stir
    to blend well. Add vinegar and spring onion greens.
6   Simmer for a minute and take off the heat. Cool and store.

TAMARIND CHUTNEY

INGREDIENTS

Tamarind (seedless) .... 1 cup
Jaggery (grated) .... 1¼ cups
Cinnamon .... 1 inch stick
Black salt .... ½ tsp
Red chilli powder .... 1 tsp

Roasted cumin powder .... 1 tsp
Dry ginger powder .... 1½ tsps
Salt .... to taste
Raisins .... 2 tbsps

METHOD OF PREPARATION

1   Soak the tamarind in two cups of water. Cook on medium heat for
    two to three minutes. Let it stand for half an hour.
2   Extract pulp by straining through a sieve. Wash the raisins and pat
    them dry.
3   Mix jaggery, cinnamon and tamarind pulp in a pan. Cook for half
    an hour on medium heat.
4   Add black salt, red chilli powder, roasted cumin powder, dry ginger
    powder and salt to taste. Cook for ten minutes.

5　Add raisins and cook for five more minutes.
6　Let cool completely and store in an airtight container.

CORIANDER AND MINT CHUTNEY

INGREDIENTS

Fresh coriander leaves .... 1 cup
Fresh mint leaves .... ½ cup
Green chillies 2-3

Black salt .... to taste
Sugar .... ¼ tsp
Lemon juice .... 1 tsp

METHOD OF PREPARATION

1   Clean, wash and roughly chop the coriander and mint leaves.
2   Remove stem, wash, de-seed and chop the green chillies.
3   In a mixer, process chopped coriander and mint leaves with chopped green chillies. Make a smooth paste using a little water if required and remove. Add salt and sugar.
4   Remove in a bowl and mix in the lemon juice.

VARIATION

Add yogurt to the chutney and mix properly (one cup of yogurt for two tablespoons of chutney).

VEGETABLE STOCK

INGREDIENTS

Onion .... 1 medium sized
Carrot .... ½ medium sized
Celery .... 2-3 inch stalk
Garlic .... 2 cloves

Bayleaf 1
Peppercorns 5-6
Cloves 2-3

METHOD OF PREPARATION

1   Peel, wash and slice onion and carrot. Wash and cut celery into small pieces. Peel and crush garlic.
2   Take all the ingredients in a pan with five cups of water and bring it to a boil.
3   Simmer for fifteen minutes and strain. Cool and store in a refrigerator till further use.

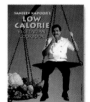

Subscribe to the most acclaimed food sites
www.sanjeevkapoor.com
and avail of unbelievable offers!!!

Pay **Rs. 500/-** only for one year subscription instead of normal subscription charges of **Rs. 1000/-** and get Sanjeev Kapoor Books worth **Rs. 750/- FREE** (only upto 31st January 2003).

You will also have access to more than 1000 recipes other than those published in his books besides many other sections, which will be a rare culinary treat to any food lover. In addition to online contests etc. you will also have opportunities to win fabulous prizes.

Sanjeev Kapoor also invites all food lovers to participate in the Khana Khazana Quiz and win BIG prizes every week. Watch Khana Khazana on Zee TV, answer one simple question based on that day's episode correctly, combine it with a favourite recipe of yours and you can be the lucky winner going places.

Subscribe to the most acclaimed food sites
www.sanjeevkapoor.com and avail of unbelievable offers

Normal Subscription	You pay	Plus you get	You save
Rs.1000	Rs.500	Sanjeev Kapoor's recipe books worth **Rs.750**	Rs.1,250

Offer open only upto 31st March, 2003

Great offer from the Khazana of Master Chef Sanjeev Kapoor.
Take your pick of book/books and avail of fantastic discounts.

Number of books	You save
1	Rs.25
2	Rs.100
More than two	Rs.200

Please tick the boxes below to indicate the books you wish to purchase

Khana Khazana
Celebration of
Indian Cooking

MRP: **Rs 250/-**

☐

Khazana Of
Indian Recipes

MRP: **Rs 250/-**

☐

Khazana Of
Healthy
Tasty Recipes

MRP: **Rs 250/-**

☐

Low Calorie
Vegetarian
Cookbook

MRP: **Rs 250/-**

☐

Any Time
Temptations

MRP: **Rs 225/-**

☐

Microwave
Cooking
Made Easy

MRP: **Rs 250/-**

☐

Best of
Chinese
Cooking

MRP: **Rs 250/-**

☐

I'm enclosing cheque/DD No. _____ dated: _____ for Rs._____

(Rupees in words): _____ only drawn on

(specify bank) _____

favouring **POPULAR PRAKASHAN PVT. LTD.,** MUMBAI.

Name: Mr./Ms.

Address:

City: Pin: State:

Phone Res: Off: E-mail: